2015

$28.50

38106000007975

781.648
ANN

D0821690

THE STORY OF
TECHNO
AND DANCE MUSIC

POP HISTORIES

MATT ANNISS

A⁺

Smart Apple Media

Published in the United States by Smart Apple Media
PO Box 3263, Mankato, Minnesota 56002

Text: Matt Anniss
Editors: Joe Harris and Rachel Blount
Design: Paul Myerscough and Keith Williams

Picture credits:
Alleviated Records: 9bl; Corbis: Steve Azzara/Sygma 11t, Karen Mason Blair 17, Classic Stock 5t, Scott Houston/Sygma 12, Fabio Nosotti 13b, Neal Preston 6l, Brittany Somerset 11b; DJhistory.com: 4, 5b; Eddie Escudero: 10b; Leighton Newell: 16; The Orb: 7t; Shutterstock: Mila Atkovska 31, Christian Bertrand 26r, 27t, Carl Bjorklund 21b, Ivan Cholakov 10t, Sam Cornwell 29, Featureflash 25r, 27b, Amy Nichole Harris 20, Rene Hartmans 14, Joyfull 19t, Anthony Mooney 1, 26l, 28, Northfoto 21t, Joe Seer 19b, Nikola Spasenoski 23r, Traxlergirl 9r; Wikipedia: 4elevenpix 24, Alkivar 15, Brandon Daniel 8, Drown 25l, Bill Ebbesen 22, GoodOmens 6r, David Koppe 23l, Wolfgang Moroder 7b, Tabanger 18, Technochick 13t.
Cover images: Dreamstime: Pressmaster main; Shutterstock: Carl Bjorklund top center left, DFree top left, Featureflash top center right, joyfull top far left; Wikipedia: Alkivar top right, Bill Ebbesen top far right.

Library of Congress Cataloging-in-Publication Data

Anniss, Matt.
 The story of techno and dance music / Matt Anniss.
     pages cm. -- (Pop histories)
Includes index.
 Summary: "Describes the beginnings and evolution of techno, dance, and electronica music, spotlighting important artists and songs"--Provided by publisher.
 ISBN 978-1-59920-967-8 (library binding)
1. Underground dance music--History and criticism--Juvenile literature. 2. Techno music--History and criticism--Juvenile literature. I. Title.
 ML3540.5.A56 2014
 781.648--dc23

                         2013003610

Printed in China

Supplier 03, Date 0513, Print Run 2373

SL002501US

CONTENTS

THE DAWN OF THE DJ

Throughout the history of the human race, people have always gathered together to dance. From early tribes moving to simple drumbeats, to medieval European maypole festivals, dancing has always been a popular pastime.

Discotheque Revolution

Dance music as we know it today has its roots in the 1970s disco scene and specifically in the "discotheques"—what we would now call nightclubs—that began in cities around the world.

The Selectors

Discotheques were different because there was no performance by a band or singer. Instead, a performer known as a "disc jockey" or "DJ" would play records. These DJs often talked in between records, and there was not much of a performance.

Disco Time

Two revolutionary DJs named Terry Noel and Francis Grasso changed everything. At a club called Salvation Too, Noel invented a technique that DJs now call "beat matching" or "mixing"—the art of seamlessly blending two songs together so that their drumbeats are perfectly in time.

FRANCIS GRASSO BECAME NEW YORK'S FIRST SUPERSTAR DJ AFTER DEVELOPING THRILLING NEW WAYS OF MIXING RECORDS TOGETHER.

Give the DJ a Break

Although it was Noel who invented mixing, it was Francis Grasso who perfected it. Grasso's style of mixing was revolutionary. He learned how to respond to the mood of dancers and would keep them entertained by mixing together the most popular parts of their favorite records.

BEAT SCIENCE

Grasso's new DJing technique was called beat matching. He would create a seamless performance by getting the beats of two records perfectly in time. Grasso's beat-matching technique quickly became popular with other DJs, and it is still the basis of all modern DJing.

DURING THE DISCO ERA, GOING OUT DANCING TO RECORDS PLAYED BY DJS BECAME MORE POPULAR THAN ATTENDING CONCERTS.

Dance Music Blueprint

As DJs in New York began to mix more, the songs they played changed. Musicians began to record disco tracks aimed at dancers, featuring drum-heavy passages that would appeal to DJs. Dance music as we know it today was starting to take shape.

TRAIL BLAZER

FRANCIS GRASSO

Francis Grasso became "resident DJ" at the Sanctuary club in the early 1970s. There, he became a local superstar, pushing a new style of DJing called mixing. Mixing quickly became a key element of all DJ performances. Grasso died in 2001, at the age of 52, but lives on through his musical influence.

THE SYNTHESIZER REVOLUTION

Just at the moment that Francis Grasso was revolutionizing the way DJs played records, another type of musical revolution was happening in a recording studio in Germany. There, a group called Kraftwerk was making music that sounded unlike anything that had gone before.

THIS "VOCODER" SYNTHESIZER WAS CUSTOM-MADE BY KRAFTWERK IN THE 1970S IN ORDER TO MAKE THEIR VOICES SOUND MORE LIKE ROBOTS.

Amazing Instrument

Up until the 1970s, nearly all music was made using traditional instruments such as guitars and drums. The invention of the synthesizer, an electronic keyboard that could be used to make futuristic sounds, changed this.

SINGER DONNA SUMMER WAS THE VOICE BEHIND SOME OF THE EARLIEST ELECTRONIC DANCE RECORDS EVER MADE.

ROBOTS AND MANNEQUINS

During the 1970s, Kraftwerk released a string of brilliant albums that introduced the world to electronic music. To further emphasize the futuristic nature of their music, they sang about being robots and dressed up to look like plastic mannequins in the windows of department stores.

Thinking Big

To start with, most musicians didn't think much of synthesizers. Kraftwerk thought differently. They believed that music made with electronic instruments such as synthesizers was the future.

ALEX PATERSON ON KRAFTWERK
[THE ORB]

"Kraftwerk were essential to the development of electronic music, particularly hip-hop and techno. The three Godfathers of Techno openly admit they were inspired by Kraftwerk."

Alex Paterson (pictured)

Enter Moroder

Another important pioneer in the 1970s was Giorgio Moroder. In 1977, he produced the first disco record created entirely using synthesizers, Donna Summer's *I Feel Love*. It was an enormous international hit and inspired many musicians to make electronic dance music.

International Hit

The work of Giorgio Moroder was important because it changed the way people made dance music. While Kraftwerk's futuristic grooves sat somewhere between pop and dance, Moroder was only interested in making people move.

Electronic Revolution

In the years that followed, electronic music began to be taken more seriously. Synthesizers and other electronic instruments became cheaper to buy, allowing bedroom musicians to turn their hand to "electro". The dance music revolution was gathering pace.

ELECTRONIC DISCO PIONEER GIORGIO MORODER, SEEN HERE IN A RECENT PICTURE, CONTINUES TO MAKE AND PRODUCE MUSIC 30 YEARS AFTER RECORDING HIS FIRST HIT.

LET THERE BE HOUSE

I t wasn't just the invention of the synthesizer that changed the course of dance music forever. In 1980, a Japanese electronics company called Roland launched a new type of drum machine called the TR-808. It would inspire a whole new generation to make dance music.

Beat the Drums

The TR-808 was revolutionary because musicians could use it to program their own drum sounds. Previously, few drum machines had this option.

Extra Beats

In the city of Chicago, Illinois, Ron Hardy and Frankie Knuckles used the Roland TR-808's drum beats to beef up the sound of the disco and electropop records they played.

Young Revolutionaries

Two local teenagers were inspired by what they heard. Jesse Saunders and Vince Lawrence, the son of a local record label owner, decided to buy their own TR-808 drum machine and create new dance tracks.

THE ROLAND TR-808 DRUM MACHINE WAS A REVOLUTIONARY INVENTION—IT ALLOWED PEOPLE WHO WEREN'T TRAINED MUSICIANS TO CREATE THEIR OWN DANCE TRACKS.

On and On

One night in 1984, Saunders and Lawrence decided to remake an old electronic disco record by Mach called *On and On*. Their version, full of what would become house music's trademark 808 drums, sounded like nothing anyone had heard before.

House Music

On and On was a big hit in Chicago's clubs and particularly at the Warehouse. It inspired a wave of similar records made with cheap drum machines such as the TR-808. Locals called it "warehouse music"—and later, "house music"—after their favorite club. Within two years, "house" was a worldwide dance floor phenomenon.

PLAYLIST
EARLY HOUSE MUSIC

Jesse Saunders—*On and On*
(Jes-Say Records, 1984)

Z-Factor feat. Jesse Saunders—*Fantasy* (instrumental) (Micthbal, 1984)

Chip-E—*Time to Jack* (Gotta Dance, 1985)

Jamie Principle—*Waiting on My Angel* (Persona, 1985)

Mr. Fingers—*Can You Feel It?* (Trax, 1986)

Frankie Knuckles—*Your Love* (Trax, 1987)

CHICAGO, ILLINOIS, WAS THE BIRTHPLACE OF HOUSE MUSIC AND CONTINUES TO PRODUCE TOP DJS AND DANCE MUSICIANS TO THIS DAY.

CHICAGO PRODUCER LARRY HEARD, BETTER KNOWN AS MR. FINGERS, ALMOST SINGLE-HANDEDLY CREATED THE DEEP HOUSE SOUND WITH HIS LEGENDARY TRACK *CAN YOU FEEL IT.*

INTO THE FUTURE

Just as the first house records were emerging in Chicago, another form of dance music was taking shape in the industrial city of Detroit. There, a group of musicians known as the Belleville Three were taking electronic music in new directions.

THE CITY OF DETROIT, MICHIGAN, ONCE FAMOUS FOR THE MASS PRODUCTION OF CARS, BECAME WELL-KNOWN IN DANCE MUSIC CIRCLES DUE TO THE EFFORTS OF EARLY TECHNO MUSICIANS SUCH AS THE BELLEVILLE THREE.

DETROIT LEGEND DERRICK MAY WAS A MEMBER OF THE BELLEVILLE THREE AND IS WIDELY REGARDED AS ONE OF THE PIONEERS OF TECHNO MUSIC.

Electro Pioneers

Juan Atkins, Derrick May, and Kevin Saunderson met while at Belleville High School. They shared a love of early electronic music. They would meet and make music in Atkins' basement using synthesizers and drum machines.

Techno City

Atkins was the first to break through. He got together with another friend, Rick Davis, and formed a band called Cybotron. They made tough electro tracks inspired by Kraftwerk, with titles such as *Clear* and *Techno City*.

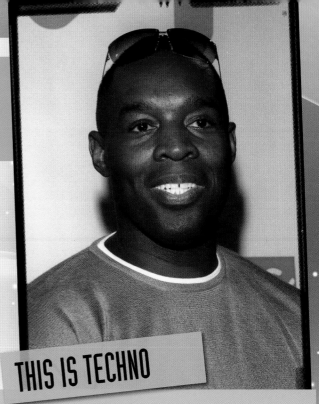

Critical Moment

The Belleville Three became well-known DJs on Detroit's underground club circuit. In 1985, they heard about the Chicago house scene and made a trip to the Warehouse to check it out for themselves.

A New Style

On returning to Detroit, all three set out to make futuristic versions of the house tracks they'd heard. In the fall of 1985, Atkins released *No UFOs* under the name Model 500. Dark and driving, it became the blueprint for a new style of dance music—techno.

Club Hits

In 1987, Derrick May released two tracks that developed the techno sound further. *Nude Photo* and *Strings of Life* were both huge international club hits. Even today, they are still considered two of the best dance records of all time.

THIS IS TECHNO

In 1988, the new techno sound of Detroit went worldwide thanks to a British compilation album. It inspired many European dance musicians to create their own versions of techno. Many of today's most popular styles of dance music, including trance, can trace their roots back to Detroit techno.

LIVING LEGEND

JUAN ATKINS

Juan Atkins is widely credited as the creator of techno music. During the mid 1990s, his futuristic productions as Model 500 and Channel One laid the foundations for today's thriving techno scene. He continues to make music, and in 2012, he released a new Model 500 single, *Control*.

11

THIS IS ACID

By 1988, the popularity of underground American dance music, particularly house and techno, had spread to Europe. There, it began to cross over into the pop charts and inspired an unlikely dance music boom.

Bad Times

The 1980s were a time of mixed fortunes for many in the UK and Europe. The divide between the rich and poor was growing all the time. Riots and political demonstrations were a common sight on the streets of major cities.

One Nation Under a Groove

Dance music helped heal these rifts. Under the influence of dance music culture, people from all walks of life began to get together at unlicensed parties called "raves".

RAVE ON

Raves were highly controversial. Although they brought people together in a "second summer of love", they were often held in farmers' fields without their permission. Because of this, governments asked the police to locate raves and shut them down.

MANY YOUNG PEOPLE IN THE UK GOT THEIR FIRST TASTE OF DANCE MUSIC AND CLUB CULTURE BY GOING TO ILLEGAL RAVES IN THE LATE 1980S AND EARLY '90S.

A GUY CALLED GERALD, SEEN HERE PERFORMING IN 2007, WAS ONE OF THE KEY PEOPLE BEHIND THE BRITISH DANCE EXPLOSION OF THE LATE 1980S.

Rock the Dance Floor

It wasn't just dance musicians who were inspired by American house and techno, either. In 1989, popular indie rock bands such as New Order, Primal Scream, and the Stone Roses began to include dance beats in their songs.

The British Scene

This dance boom also inspired British and European teenagers to try their hand at making what was now called "acid house". Thanks to the work of acts such as A Guy Called Gerald, the KLF, and 808 State, a homegrown British dance scene developed.

Mainstream Scene

Leading pop bands such as the Pet Shop Boys—and in the UK, the Style Council—also enjoyed hits with cover versions of well-loved acid house songs. Acid house was now part of the mainstream.

PLAYLIST
ACID HOUSE

Sterling Void—*It's All Right* (DJ International, 1987)

T-Coy—*Carino* (Deconstruction, 1987)

A Guy Called Gerald—*Voodoo Ray* (Rham, 1988)

808 State—*Let Yourself Go* (Creed, 1988)

Raze—*Break 4 Love* (Grove Street, 1988)

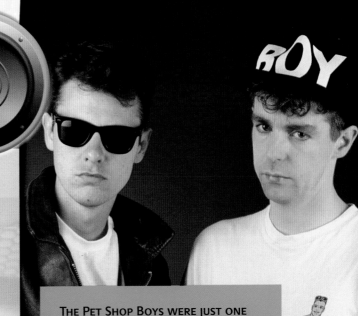

THE PET SHOP BOYS WERE JUST ONE OF A NUMBER OF POP BANDS THAT WERE INSPIRED BY THE POPULARITY OF DANCE MUSIC IN THE EARLY 1990S.

13

HARDCORE UPROAR

The UK rave scene of the late 1980s inspired many young people to buy cheap drum machines and synthesizers and make their own dance music. The result was a period of great change, as new styles began to take shape.

Culture Clash

The musical influences on young British musicians were often very different to those of their American counterparts. Those growing up in big cities were often surrounded by the sounds played by black immigrants, such as reggae.

Bleep and Bass

It wasn't long before sounds from these styles began appearing in British dance tracks. In 1990, a style developed called "bleep techno". This fused reggae-style bass with the futuristic sounds of Detroit.

HARDCORE REVOLUTION

Another key development around that time was "breakbeat hardcore". Its beats were looser and more hectic than those used on house and techno records. Developed in the UK rather than the United States, it helped launch the careers of now-famous dance acts such as Orbital and the Prodigy.

BEFORE THEY BECAME GLOBAL DANCE SUPERSTARS, THE PRODIGY MADE THEIR NAME BY MAKING UNDERGROUND BREAKBEAT HARDCORE RECORDS.

On a Ragga Tip

Many breakbeat hardcore records also borrowed basslines from Jamaican styles such as reggae and "ragga". In the early 1990s, SL2 and Shut Up & Dance enjoyed huge success with songs that mixed rave and ragga.

Speed It Up

In 1992, two DJs named Fabio and Grooverider started speeding up the hardcore records they played. It was a revolutionary moment. Soon, producers in London started creating faster hardcore records.

Jungle Music

This new style of music was called "jungle". By the time it became widely popular in the mid 1990s, it had a new name: drum and bass. Today, drum and bass is one of the most popular forms of dance music around the world.

INSIDE THE SOUND

JUNGLE

Jungle, which later became drum and bass, differs from house and techno in three ways. First, it is based around "breakbeats", which have more swing than the rigid beats used in house and techno. Second, it uses big basslines inspired by reggae music. Third, it is significantly faster than both house and techno.

By speeding up breakbeat hardcore records in his DJ sets, Grooverider inspired the creation of a whole new style called jungle.

CHILL-OUT

Not all electronic music in the early 1990s was as fast as hardcore or jungle. Around the same time, a style of music called "chill-out" emerged. It was slow and supposed to be listened to while lying down.

Made in Heaven

The roots of chill-out music lie in an underground London club called Heaven. The club had two rooms. As an alternative to the main room's dance sounds, the second featured slow music for clubbers who wanted a rest from dancing.

Ambient House

The DJs in the second room were a pair of friends named Jimmy Cauty and Alex Paterson. In 1989, they made their own chill-out record as the Orb. It was the start of the "ambient house" movement.

Chill-out

The album that put ambient house on the map was *Chill Out* by the KLF, of which Cauty was a member. Combining slow, hypnotic synthesizer loops with sound effects and snatches of famous records, it was something of an underground hit.

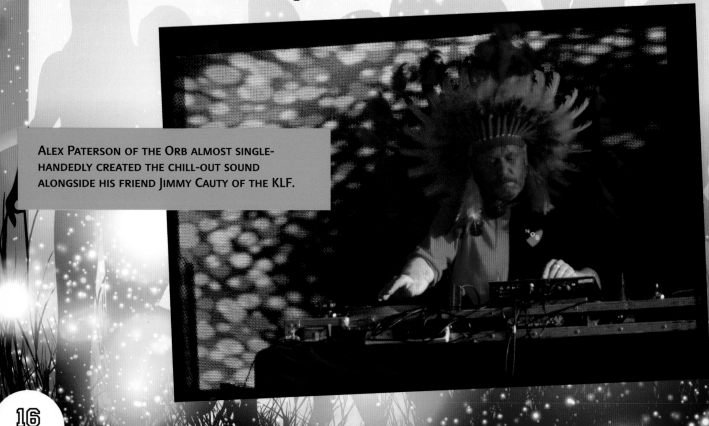

ALEX PATERSON OF THE ORB ALMOST SINGLE-HANDEDLY CREATED THE CHILL-OUT SOUND ALONGSIDE HIS FRIEND JIMMY CAUTY OF THE KLF.

Elsewhere around the world, other musicians were experimenting with slow or unusual electronic music. This would become known as "intelligent dance music", or IDM for short.

Ambient House Superstar

Without Jimmy Cauty, Alex Paterson went on to record many successful albums as the Orb. Mixing slow ambient sounds with dub reggae and slowed-down techno beats, the Orb became one of the most popular dance acts of the 1990s.

Home Listening

IDM, now known as electronica, showed that electronic music could be about more than heavy dance floor rhythms. It was designed for home listening—something for clubbers to check out when they got home from raves.

Enter Aphex Twin

One of the most successful IDM producers of the period was Aphex Twin. His music still influences musicians today. The rock band Radiohead, for instance, started making electronica after listening to Aphex Twin albums.

INDIE BAND RADIOHEAD STARTED MAKING ELECTRONICA RECORDS AFTER HEARING THE EXPERIMENTAL IDM SOUNDS OF APHEX TWIN.

PLAYLIST
CLASSIC ELECTRONICA

The KLF—*Madrugada Eterna* (KLF Communications, 1990)

The Orb – *Little Fluffy Clouds* (Big Life, 1990)

The Black Dog—*Parallel* (General Production, 1991)

System 7—*Altitude* (10, 1991)

Aphex Twin – *On* (Warp, 1993)

030—*Midnight in Europe* (MFS, 1993)

17

GOING LIVE

During the 1990s, the popularity of electronic music soared. Both dance and electronica were big business. Soon, there was huge demand for the most popular acts to play live.

Rare Performances

The first live performances from electronic bands took place in the 1970s, with Kraftwerk leading the way. However, up until the early 1990s, they were a rare occurrence.

Festival Frenzy

All that changed when dance and electronica acts became famous during the rave era. The popularity of these bands was such that organizers of music festivals, traditionally a place only for rock acts, started to ask them to appear.

Live and Direct

Changes in music technology allowed electronic musicians to recreate their tracks, note for note, on stage. Before, it would have been almost impossible. Now, they could put on impressive performances and even remix their songs during their sets.

WITH ROOTS IN INDIE-ROCK, UNDERWORLD WERE ONE OF THE FIRST 1990S DANCE ACTS TO ENJOY SUCCESS ON THE LIVE CONCERT CIRCUIT.

Dance Festivals

In the years that followed, more dance acts enhanced their reputations through energetic live performances. In Europe, at dedicated dance festivals such as Homelands and Global Gathering, dancers were entertained with sets from the Chemical Brothers, Daft Punk, Underworld, and Basement Jaxx.

Lots of Performers

Nowadays, there is nothing particularly surprising about seeing your favorite dance acts play live. In recent years, Pendulum, Justice, and Modeselektor have built their reputations on dazzling live shows, while original pioneers Kraftwerk have come out of retirement to play at festivals.

Blurred Boundaries

Today, computer technology exists that allows DJs to recreate their own music live. Top DJs such as Paul Van Dyk and Tiësto now play sets that blur the boundaries between traditional DJing and live performance.

THE CHEMICAL BROTHERS

The Chemical Brothers are arguably the most successful live dance act of all time. They first played live in 1995 and have since headlined many music festivals around the world. In 2012, one of their shows was released as a movie, *Don't Think*.

DAFT PUNK USE FLASHING ROBOT MASKS TO HIDE THEIR IDENTITY AND ADD INTEREST TO THEIR IMPRESSIVE LIVE SHOWS.

SUPERSTAR DJS, HERE WE GO!

During the late 1990s, the unsung heroes of dance music made a comeback. Having started the dance music revolution in the 1970s, DJs were back in fashion. Now, they were replacing rock singers as music's biggest superstars.

Central Figures

DJs had always been a critical part of dance music culture. Before the advent of live dance acts, they were the people who provided the soundtrack to nights out all around the world. They were also tastemakers, able to make or break new records—shaping the dance scene.

Making Music

Many DJs were also musicians. Throughout the rave revolution, it was the DJs who made many of the most popular dance tracks. Since they knew what appealed to dancers, they had a head start on regular musicians.

The Producers

The 1990s saw a rise in DJ producers—club DJs who also became famous for making music. Sasha, Paul Oakenfold, and Paul Van Dyk, one of the founders of the trance sound, all became international superstars on the back of playing and making music.

DURING THE LATE 1990S AND EARLY 2000S, TRANCE PIONEER PAUL VAN DYK WAS ONE OF THE MOST POPULAR SUPERSTAR DJS ON THE PLANET.

BIG BEAT HERO

The biggest DJ superstar of all was Norman Cook, better known as Fatboy Slim. After making his name with a string of chart hits, he quickly became famous for his energetic and exciting DJ sets. Demand to see him perform was huge; in 2002, he played to 250,000 people on Brighton beach in the UK.

Still Superstars

In recent years, demand for superstar DJs has fallen, but there are a few big names that can still fill arenas. Tiësto, Armin Van Buuren, David Guetta, and Paul Oakenfold have all become millionaires on the back of their DJing work.

LIVING LEGEND

TIËSTO

Dutch trance DJ Tiësto first rose to prominence in the late 1990s. By the early 2000s, he was so popular that he was named the world's number one DJ three years in a row. In 2004, he performed a DJ set live to a global audience of billions at the Athens Olympics.

PANIC AT THE DISCO!

By the mid 2000s, the popularity of dance and electronic music was declining. While the underground scene remained healthy, going to nightclubs didn't hold the same attraction to young people as it once had. Dance was in trouble.

Lost Generation

During the 1990s, dance music was incredibly popular with young people, but by the middle of the 2000s, this had changed. College students, previously the loudest supporters of the dance scene, were now more interested in indie and rock music.

Lone Voices

Some indie and rock bands, though, still held dance music and electronica in high regard. Radiohead, once darlings of the Britpop indie-rock scene, continued to make electronica records.

BACK TO NEW YORK

Elsewhere, things were slowly changing, too. Over in New York, a record label called DFA (short for Death From Above) were creating exciting new musical fusions inspired by 1970s disco, post-punk rock, and 1980s house music.

NEW YORK BAND LCD SOUNDSYSTEM WERE ONE OF THE FIRST BANDS TO FUSE POST-PUNK ROCK WITH MODERN DANCE MUSIC.

MEMBERS OF INDIE-DANCE ACT HOT CHIP LIKE DANCE MUSIC SO MUCH THAT THEY MAKE HOUSE MUSIC IN THEIR SPARE TIME!

New Rave

In 2006, a new indie-dance sound began to emerge. Spearheaded by bands such as the Klaxons and Justice, "new rave" soon became hugely popular, particularly with students. It was loud, heavy, and tons of fun.

Lasting Legacy

New rave was short-lived, but it has left a lasting legacy. Not only is indie-dance now one of the most popular forms of music, but it also helped a whole new generation fall in love with going out dancing.

Murphy's Law

The man behind DFA was a musician named James Murphy. James, with his band LCD Soundsystem, did much to breathe new life into both rock and dance music. In the second half of the 2000s, LCD Soundsystem was at the forefront of dance/rock fusion.

Hot Band

Other bands around the world were excited by the potential of "indie-dance" and "dance-rock". One of the most successful UK indie bands of recent years, Hot Chip, led the way.

INSIDE THE SOUND
NEW RAVE

New rave emerged when a group of indie-rock bands began to make pop songs that mixed loud guitar riffs with dance music beats and sounds. Often, the drums and synthesizers they used sounded like the hardcore breakbeat records of the early 1990s.

BASS, HOW LOW CAN YOU GO?

While indie-dance was breathing new life into the dance music scene, another new style was beginning to make its mark. Over the next few years, dubstep would go on to dominate dance floors around the world.

THROUGH HIS EARLY RELEASES ON BIG APPLE RECORDS, LONDON PRODUCER PLASTICIAN HELPED DEFINE THE DUBSTEP SOUND.

Garage Roots

Many of today's biggest dubstep stars, such as Skrillex, hail from the United States. However, to begin with, it was a very British phenomenon. It originally developed out of a popular British style of music called "2-step garage".

GARAGE HISTORY

UK garage, or 2-step garage, was popular in the late 1990s. It was funky, upbeat, and bass-heavy. It used a particular type of "2-step" beat pattern that differed from American garage, which used beats similar to house music.

Baby Steps

Some musicians and DJs in London were tired of the upbeat positivity of 2-step garage. They started making darker, moodier records, emphasizing the heavy basslines. By 2003, the beat patterns had changed and a new style emerged—dubstep.

Giant Strides

Thanks to the work of pioneering DJs and producers such as DMZ, Plastician, Skream, and Horsepower Productions, dubstep soon became popular. It wasn't long before dubstep club nights began popping up around the world.

Bass Anthems

As the 2000s progressed, dubstep gained in popularity. Its biggest DJs began touring the world, playing to large audiences in America, Australia, and New Zealand. Skream, Roska, and Skrillex proved the pop potential of the sound by recording dance anthems.

Global Bass

Now, the bass music scene around the world is stronger than it has ever been. Elements of dubstep can be heard in pop songs, techno records, and even some of the biggest house records of recent years.

AMERICAN DJ SKRILLEX WAS THE FIRST DUBSTEP PRODUCER TO ACHIEVE SUPERSTAR STATUS AROUND THE WORLD.

SKREAM WAS ONE OF THE FIRST DUBSTEP DJs TO RISE TO INTERNATIONAL PROMINENCE.

Bass Revival

Dubstep's popularity also helped create interest in other forms of bass music. Drum and bass and UK garage also made a comeback, while young DJs began to play old hardcore and jungle records.

PLAYLIST
THE ROOTS OF DUBSTEP

Dub War—*Murderous Style* (Tempa, 2001)

Maddslinky—*Desert Fog* (Sirkus, 2001)

Horsepower Productions—*Fists of Fury* (Tempa, 2001)

Artwork—*Red* (Big Apple, 2002)

Mark One vs. Plasticman – *Hard Graft* (White, 2003)

Benga & Skream—*The Judgement* (Big Apple, 2003)

HEROES OF THE POP CHARTS

The crossover success of dubstep and drum and bass may have taken some by surprise. However, house music's continuing dominance of the pop charts is less surprising. Since the 1990s, house music has been big business.

Pop Means Popular

Due to its long history and early links with popular musical forms such as soul and disco, house music has always been at the forefront of what some describe as "dance-pop". This is dance music designed to appeal to pop music listeners.

DANCE-POP IS SO POPULAR THAT CONCERTS BY MAJOR BANDS AND SINGERS OFTEN SELL OUT WITHIN HOURS.

Electro Origins

Many dance-pop stars emerge from the underground house scene. From the mid 2000s to the present day, most superstar pop-dance DJs and producers have emerged from the electro house scene. This is the route that the Swedish House Mafia took to the top.

THE BLACK EYED PEAS' WILL.I.AM IS THE UNDISPUTED MASTER OF DANCE-POP, HAVING SWITCHED FROM MAKING RAP MUSIC IN THE EARLY 1990S.

Things Can Only Get Guetta

The man who has done most to push dance-pop forward is a DJ producer named David Guetta. He had been a house DJ in Paris, France, since the 1980s but found fame in the 2000s after creating a series of hit dance-pop singles.

Big Name Guests

The success of Guetta and the Swedish House Mafia has been such that they have been able to work with some of the biggest rappers and singers on the planet. Between them, they have worked with Usher, Rhianna, Tinie Tempa, Chris Brown, and Lil' Wayne.

Superstars of Pop

The continued popularity of dance-pop songs is reflected in the type of records major R & B and hip-hop stars have been making. In recent years, Beyoncé, Snoop Dogg, and the Black Eyed Peas have all scored huge hits with dance-pop songs.

Radio Revival

The popularity of dance-pop in the United States has led to another significant change. For years, American radio stations ignored dance music. Now, many are playing dance tracks alongside pop and R & B records.

LIVING LEGEND

DAVID GUETTA

French DJ producer David Guetta released his first album, *Just a Little More Love*, in 2002. Since then, he has become one of the best-selling dance producers of all time, selling over 3 million albums and 15 million singles.

27

DANCE PLANET

In the 40 years since New York DJ Francis Grasso kick-started the DJing revolution, dance music has grown and changed beyond recognition. What started out in a handful of American cities has now become a genuine global music force.

From Small Beginnings

When Jesse Saunders and Vince Lawrence created their first house track in Chicago in 1984, they could never have imagined that the style would become a key part of pop music in the twenty-first century.

CONSTANT CHANGE

As dance music has spread around the world, many new styles have emerged in different places. In Eastern Europe, fast Euro-dance has been mixed with traditional local styles to make turbo-folk. Indian bhangra music has been mixed with hip-hop and dance beats to create "folkhop".

Global Soundtrack

The same can be said of many other dance and electronic styles, from electronica, IDM, and rave, to jungle, dubstep, and indie-dance. What was once the preserve of a few teenagers in underground clubs has become the soundtrack to our daily lives.

IN THE TWENTY-FIRST CENTURY, DANCING ALL NIGHT IN TOP CLUBS HAS BECOME A REGULAR PASTIME FOR YOUNG PEOPLE ALL OVER THE WORLD.

African Rhythms

In South Africa, DJ producers have created a new fusion of traditional African music and Western electronica called Shangan Electro. Meanwhile, African immigrants in Portugal have developed "progressive kuduro", which fuses Afrobeat rhythms with house and techno.

Evolution

Throughout the world, dance music continues to evolve, as it always has done. DJs and musicians can now take influences from 40 years of dance music, push them together, and create thrilling new styles. The latest dance hot spot is Mexico, where musicians are making "new wave" music that mixes disco, rock, house, techno, funk, and soul.

Revival

Disco, house, and techno, dance music's oldest forms, continue to form the basis of new styles. In recent years, variants such as tech house, dub techno, and nu-disco have all proved hugely popular. Times may change, but our desire to dance to new music will remain.

PLAYLIST
GLOBAL DANCE MUSIC

Buraka Som Sistema— *Sound of Kuduro* (Portugal, 2007)

DJ Mujava— *Township Funk* (South Africa, 2008)

Gramaphonedzie— *Krejzau* (Serbia, 2009)

Edu K— *Popozuda Rock N" Roll* (Brazil, 2009)

Tshetshe Boys— *Nwa Pfundla* (South Africa, 2010)

Moonrunner— *Interactive Track* (Mexico, 2012)

GLOSSARY

bass The low sounds that underpin most dance, pop, rock, and hip-hop records.

compilation An album that gathers together songs from many different musicians.

crossover A term to describe a record or style of music that has emerged out of the "underground" to become widely popular.

disco A style of upbeat dance music that originated in the 1970s, based on soul.

drum machine A piece of electronic equipment used to create drumbeats.

electro A style of house music that uses heavy electronic sounds.

electronica The name given to any type of electronic music not made to be played in clubs.

electropop Also known as synth-pop, this is a style of pop music created using electronic instruments such as synthesizers.

evolved Changed over time.

fused Joined together.

garage A style of bass-heavy music popular in the UK. Sometimes called "2-step garage" or "UK garage".

IDM Short for "intelligent dance music".

influence Something or someone that inspires other people, for instance, by creating a new style of music.

mixing The process of blending songs together to create a DJ performance.

pioneering Doing something first.

program To create something using a computer or other electronic equipment, for example, a drum machine or synthesizer.

reggae A slow, bass-heavy style of music that originated in Jamaica.

revolutionary Something that is so significant that it changes the way people do things or the way we live.

rhythm A pattern of drumbeats. Also used to refer to the speed and style of a track.

synthesizer An electronic keyboard.

trance A popular style of dance music that evolved from techno in the late 1980s and early 1990s.

underground A scene or style that is not well-known and is usually only popular with enthusiasts.

FURTHER INFORMATION

Further Reading

House Music: The Real Story by Jesse Saunders and Jason Cummins (PublishAmerica, 2007)

On the Record: The Scratch DJ Academy Guide by Luke Crisell, Rob Principe, and Phil White (St. Martin's Griffin, 2009)

The Record Players: DJ Revolutionaries by Brian Brewster and Frank Broughton (Grove Press, Black Cat, 2011)

Superstar DJs Here We Go! The Rise and Fall of the Superstar DJ by Dom Phillips (Ebury Press, 2009)

Web Sites

www.dubspot.com
Web site of Dubspot, DJ and Music Production School in New York City and online. Great tutorial videos for DJ software, tips, mixing, and mastering. With artist profiles and interviews.

www.fastcodesign.com/1665393/
infographic-of-the-day-the-history-of-
dance-music-in-one-handy-timeline
View graphics explaining how dance music has spread, expanded, and changed over the last 40 years on this great site.

www.usadanceradio.com
Internet radio station that plays all types of dance music, from classic dance and techno to trance.

INDEX